Cornerstones of Freedom

Women's Voting Rights

Miles Harvey

CHILDREN'S PRESS®
A Division of Grolier Publishing
New York • London • Hong Kong • Sydney
Danbury, Connecticut

Library of Congress Cataloging-in-Publication Data

Harvey, Miles.
    Women's voting rights / by Miles Harvey.
        p. cm. — (Cornerstones of freedom)
    Includes index.
    ISBN 0-516-20003-8
    1. Women—Suffrage—United States—History—Juvenile
literature. I. Title. II. Series.
JK1898.H37 1996
324.6'23'0973—dc20
                                                    96-5068
                                                        CIP
                                                        AC

On November 2, 1920, Americans from all over the country went to the polls to elect a president. Such elections were nothing new. They had been taking place regularly since George Washington became the first U.S. president in 1789. But this year, something was dramatically different.

Women who called themselves "suffragettes" campaigning for the right to vote in Cleveland, Ohio

For the first time ever, all women across the country were allowed to vote.

The right to vote is called suffrage. For the first 144 years of this country's existence, women did not have that right. The story of how they got it is one of the most fascinating and important chapters in American history.

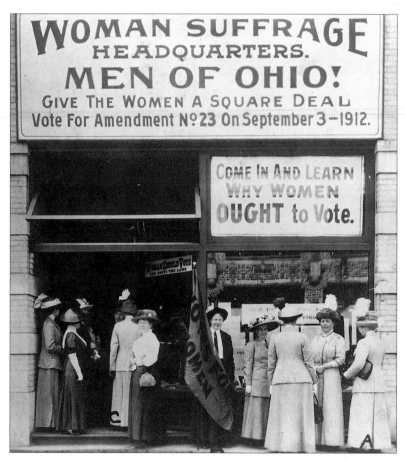

This story began before the United States was a country and even before European colonists arrived in North America. In American Indian societies, women played important roles. Among the Iroquois Indians, for example, women got to vote in the election of male leaders. And among the Cherokee, women had the right to speak at village meetings, where important decisions were made.

White people began to settle large sections of North America during the seventeenth century. Many of them came in search of freedom. In 1620, the Pilgrims sailed on the *Mayflower* from England to what is now Plymouth, Massachusetts. They wanted the freedom to practice their religion. Others came because they wanted freedom to start their own farms and businesses.

The right to worship was very important to the Pilgrims.

North American colonists discussed important colonial issues and worshiped in a common meetinghouse.

Another important freedom to these settlers was democracy. In a democracy, people get to choose their own leaders. Democracy was a pretty new concept in the seventeenth century. Before that time, kings and queens ran European countries without any say from their citizens. But beginning in 1642, people in England demanded that they have a stronger voice in the affairs of their government. As a result, England became more democratic. The country did not get rid of its king, but it did give strong powers to politicians who were elected by citizens.

When English colonists came to America, they brought the idea of democracy with them. All of the colonies had some kind of regional elections, and people who owned property were permitted to participate. In those days, most women were not allowed to own land. So only in very rare cases were they allowed to vote.

One person who believed this system was unfair was Margaret Brent. Not only was she one of the few colonial women of the seventeenth century to own her own property, but she also took care of her own finances. She even helped men with their business affairs.

In 1648, Brent shocked many people in colonial Maryland when she demanded the right to vote. She argued that because she owned property, she should be able to participate in elections. Maryland officials didn't agree. They told her that she would be unable to vote because she was a woman. Despite this disappointment, Margaret Brent went down in history as the first American woman to insist on full participation in the democratic process.

In the colonies, male voters didn't always have the advantage. Colonists were not allowed to vote on members of Parliament, the group of elected English politicians that made laws for America. They also had to pay large amounts of tax money to England and its king. As the years went on, Americans became angrier and angrier about what they called "taxation without representation." They wanted a say in government, and they were willing to fight to get it.

In 1775, the Revolutionary War began. A year later, leaders from all over the colonies signed one of the most famous documents in history. It was called the Declaration of Independence. On

July 4, 1776, the Declaration created a new country—the United States of America. To this day, U.S. citizens still celebrate every Fourth of July as the nation's birthday.

The Declaration of Independence spelled out the basic ideas of democracy. For example, it said that a government must have "the consent of the governed." In other words, the leaders of a country must be chosen by the people. The Declaration also said that "all men are created equal." This meant that no group of citizens should get special privileges denied to other groups.

But this did not apply to women, because women were not generally considered citizens. To be a citizen, a person had to own property. And once a woman married, she had to give all her money, land, and possessions to her husband. In fact, the wife herself was usually thought to be her husband's property.

Women weren't the only people who were denied citizenship. White men who did not own land were also excluded from politics. So were American Indians. And African-American slaves had no rights of any kind, including the right to vote.

Thus, the Declaration of Independence did not mean real independence or equality for all Americans. But it did inspire people to try to achieve those ideals. As the years passed, the Declaration became a symbol of hope for African-Americans, women, and other groups as they struggled to gain equal rights as citizens.

African-American slaves were treated as property by wealthy landowners.

Even at the time of the Revolutionary War, a small number of people were pushing for women's rights. One of them was journalist Thomas Paine, whose powerful writings inspired thousands of colonists to revolt against England. In 1775, a publication

edited by Paine called *Pennsylvania Magazine* said that women should have the same rights as men.

Abigail Smith Adams, the wife of future U.S. president John Adams, was another supporter of women's rights. In 1776, she wrote to her husband, "Remember the Ladies . . . [or we] will not hold ourselves bound by any laws in which we have no voice or representation."

But John Adams and the other politicians who helped create the new government ignored such ideas. In 1789, the U.S. Constitution was established as the basic set of rules by which the new country would operate. The Constitution described the way citizens would elect presidents and members of the two branches of Congress, the House of Representatives and the Senate. But women, along with African-Americans, American Indians, and many poor people, were still not considered full citizens. That meant they couldn't vote.

New Jersey was the only state that allowed women to participate in elections. Beginning in 1783, women who owned a certain amount of property were allowed to vote in New Jersey. But by 1807, women were once again excluded from elections.

Nonetheless, more and more women were beginning to wonder why they did not have the same rights as men. In 1792, English author Mary Wollstonecraft published an important book called *A Vindication of the Rights of Woman*. Wollstonecraft wrote that the American people had been justified in their revolt against unfair treatment by England. Now, she argued, it was time for women to rise up against the unfair way they were treated by men.

Mary Wollstonecraft's ideas were unconventional for her time. She believed that women should have the same rights as men.

Lucretia Mott

Wollstonecraft's book inspired many American women. Among them were Lucretia Mott and Elizabeth Cady Stanton. These two women became important leaders in a new political movement that would later become known as feminism.

Mott was born in 1793. After she grew up, she became a minister in the Quaker church. Like many Quakers, Mott was strongly opposed to the enslavement of African-Americans. She became an important leader in the antislavery movement in the United States. Elizabeth Cady Stanton was

Quakers believe in equality between men and women. Here, a Quaker woman preaches to a crowd.

more than twenty years younger than Mott. But like Mott, Stanton was determined to end slavery.

Stanton and Mott met each other in 1840 at an antislavery conference in London, England. The two women had traveled all the way across the Atlantic Ocean thinking that women would be able to participate in the conference. But as the event got underway, male antislavery leaders voted to keep women out of the meeting even though some women had been elected as delegates. This made Stanton and Mott very angry. They decided that from then on, they would work on behalf of equal rights for women as well as for blacks.

In 1848, Mott and Stanton organized the first women's rights convention in America. They held the meeting, attended by both women and men, near Stanton's home in Seneca Falls, New York. At the end of the two-day event, conference participants published the "Declaration of Sentiments." The document was based on the Declaration of Independence. But instead of claiming that "all men are created equal," the Declaration of Sentiments said that "all men and women are created equal." It also argued that women deserved the right to vote.

Elizabeth Cady Stanton

This pamphlet is from the first women's rights convention in the United States. One editorial called the meeting "the most shocking and unnatural incident ever recorded in the history of womanity."

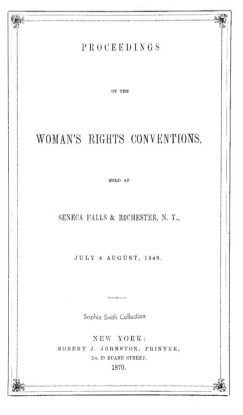

PROCEEDINGS

OF THE

WOMAN'S RIGHTS CONVENTIONS.

HELD AT

SENECA FALLS & ROCHESTER, N. Y.,

JULY & AUGUST, 1848.

Sophia Smith Collection

NEW YORK:
ROBERT J. JOHNSTON, PRINTER,
No. 39 DUANE STREET.
1870.

Susan B. Anthony was once called "The Woman Who Dared."

In 1860, the New York state legislature granted women certain rights. But, as this sign indicates, it was a tough battle to win the right to vote.

In 1851, Elizabeth Cady Stanton met a woman named Susan B. Anthony. Stanton and Anthony soon began working together for women's rights. They made a perfect team. Stanton had the ability to inspire people with her words and thoughts. Anthony had great planning and organizational skills. She could take Stanton's ideas and turn them into action. With Stanton and Anthony as two of its top leaders, the feminist movement began to gain popularity across the United States.

In 1854, Stanton became the first woman to give a major speech to the New York state legislature. She called on lawmakers to grant women basic legal rights. At that time, a woman's husband owned all her property. And if a couple got divorced, the wife had no say about who got custody of their children. Stanton argued that these rules were unfair. And slowly, she and Anthony began to convince politicians of their case.

In 1860, the New York state legislature passed a law that gave married women the rights to keep their own property, to earn wages, and to have a say about who got the children in case of a divorce. Soon, other states began passing similar laws.

These laws gave women much more control over their lives. In the years that followed, more and more women began working in businesses and going to college. But Stanton and Anthony knew that women would never be truly equal to men until they could vote and be elected to public office. So in 1866, Stanton became the first woman to run for a seat in the U.S. Congress. She didn't stand a chance of winning, but she ran to show that women were determined to be involved in American democracy.

During the Civil War (1861–65), Stanton and Anthony strongly supported the U.S. government in its battle against the South. They also campaigned on behalf of the Thirteenth Amendment to the Constitution, to end slavery in the United States. When the amendment passed in 1865, Stanton and Anthony hoped that both African-Americans and women would be given the right to vote.

They were deeply disappointed. In 1868, the Fourteenth Amendment passed, defining citizenship and giving all male citizens the right to vote. This was the first time the Constitution specifically said that only men could vote.

Politicians began to discuss adding a Fifteenth Amendment. The proposed amendment was intended to ensure voting rights for African-American men. It said that no one could be denied the right to vote on account of "race, color, or previous condition of servitude." But the word "sex" was not included on the list. Stanton and Anthony were mad. After all, adding that one small word would have meant full citizenship for women all over the country.

With the passage of the Fifteenth Amendment, all African-American men were allowed to vote, even if they were former slaves.

Lucy Stone

Julia Ward Howe

Stanton and Anthony decided to speak out against the passage of the Fifteenth Amendment. But other important feminist leaders, such as Lucy Stone and Julia Ward Howe, did not agree with Stanton and Anthony. Stone and Howe believed that voting rights for African-Americans would eventually lead to voting rights for women. They also criticized Stanton and Anthony for accepting money from racists who were more interested in denying blacks voting rights than in helping women.

In 1869, the feminist movement broke into two separate groups. Stanton and Anthony formed the National Woman Suffrage Association, which opposed passage of the Fifteenth Amendment. Stone and Howe formed the American Woman Suffrage Association, which supported the amendment. The Fifteenth

Amendment became law in 1870, but hard feelings between the two organizations lasted for many years afterward.

Despite the split, the suffrage movement continued to gain popularity. In 1872, the Republican Party—then the leading political group in the country—mentioned its "obligation to the loyal women of America." That same year, Victoria Woodhull became the first woman to run for president of the United States. Many women across the country attempted to vote, even though it was illegal. One of them was Susan B. Anthony, who was arrested after she cast her ballot in Rochester, New York. A judge later fined her one hundred dollars, which she refused to pay.

In 1872, Victoria Woodhull became the first woman to run for president of the United States.

The National Woman's Suffrage Association campaigned for a women's suffrage amendment.

In 1873, many women in the Midwest began to hold large public protests. These women were not demonstrating in favor of equal rights. Instead, they were angry that their husbands and other men spent so much time in bars. They wanted to make it illegal to drink alcohol in the United States. This effort was known as the "temperance movement." In 1874, a national group called the Woman's Christian

The temperance movement was also called the "women's whisky war." Here, women in Indiana demolish a cargo of liquor at the railroad depot.

18

Temperance Union was formed. During the next few years, hundreds of thousands of women joined the group. Women tried to prevent men from drinking by writing down names of the men at saloons and singing hymns outside. Men would try to drive them away with skunks.

Women in the temperance movement quickly became frustrated with the way that some male politicians ignored their demands. They realized that if they were to succeed, they would need the power of the vote. As a result, many women in the temperance movement joined forces with the suffrage movement on the issue of voting rights.

With support for its cause on the rise, the National Woman Suffrage Association was able to collect ten thousand signatures from Americans demanding the right to vote for women. In 1877, Susan B. Anthony delivered these signatures to the U.S. Senate. But lawmakers were still not willing to take the women's rights movement seriously. They greeted Anthony with loud laughter.

Anthony and the other feminist leaders did not let such teasing bother them. In 1878, they persuaded one senator to propose an amendment to the Constitution that would give women the right to vote. It did not pass. But its supporters planned to introduce the proposal every year until it became law.

Meanwhile, the suffrage cause continued to gain strength. In 1890, the National Woman Suffrage Association and the American Woman Suffrage Association finally settled their disagreements. They came together in a new group called the National American Woman Suffrage Association. That same year, the new state of Wyoming became the first in the country to allow women the right to vote. Three years later, Colorado also granted women suffrage. And in 1896, Utah and Idaho became the third and fourth states to give women equal rights at the polls. The movement was also making progress in other countries. In 1893, New Zealand became the first modern country in which all women could vote.

In 1900, when Susan B. Anthony was eighty years old, she retired as president of the National American Woman Suffrage Association. She supported the election of Carrie Chapman Catt to replace her. Like Anthony, Catt was brilliant at organizing political events and campaigns. In a few years, hard work by Catt and other leaders, such as

Women Vote in 12 States

Give the Vote to the Women of Massachusetts in November 1915

Mothers need the Vote to Protect their Homes and Children.

Working Women need the Vote to regulate conditions under which they work.

Tax paying Women need the Vote to Protect their Property.

THINK IT OVER!

By the courtesy of the Woman's Journal, Boston.

State by state, women were slowly gaining support.

*Women at the polls
in Wyoming*

Anna Howard Shaw and Jane Addams, started
to pay off. In 1910, Washington became the
first state in fourteen years to give women
the right to vote. A number of other states
quickly followed.

Some women thought that these changes
were happening too slowly. These women
believed that radical tactics were necessary.
In 1913, they formed a group called the
Congressional Union, which later became
the National Woman's Party. The group was
led by Alice Paul. Paul was not interested in
politely discussing the suffrage cause with
male politicians. Instead, she believed that
the only way to win these men over was to
intimidate and embarrass them.

*Carrie Chapman
Catt*

Alice Paul

So Alice Paul and her friends began a campaign aimed at forcing male politicians to support women's rights. For many months, they held round-the-clock protests in front of the White House, sometimes chaining themselves to the fence. When they were arrested, which was

This suffragette calls on the president to pay attention to her cause.

often, they refused to eat. Some other feminists felt embarrassed by these tactics and predicted that they wouldn't work. But Paul and her friends proved their critics wrong. Their protests received a lot of publicity in newspapers and created increased support for the suffrage movement. Many politicians— including President Woodrow Wilson— eventually came out in support of voting rights for women.

President Woodrow Wilson supported women's right to vote.

This humorous photo from 1901 shows that men were scared they would lose their traditional leadership roles in the home as women redefined their roles in society.

These politicians understood that the world was changing quickly. In the late 1800s and early 1900s, millions of American women were working at jobs outside the home, and thousands more were attending college. Large numbers of women had economic power—and now they wanted political power.

On January 10, 1918, a woman named Jeannette Rankin addressed the House of Representatives. Rankin was from Montana, one of the states where women could vote and hold office. Two years earlier, she had become the first woman in history to be elected to the U.S. Congress. Now she was introducing an amendment to the Constitution that would give all American women the right to full citizenship.

Jeannette Rankin was the nation's first congresswoman.

The same proposal had been introduced in Congress every year since 1878. It had always lost. But this year, support was strong, and it finally had a good chance of winning. The amendment barely passed the House of Representatives by the necessary two-thirds vote. That was a big first step. To become law, the amendment now had to be passed by two-thirds of the Senate, then approved by three-fourths of the states.

Carrie Chapman Catt, Alice Paul, and thousands of other women immediately went back to work. It took them more than two years, but on August 26, 1920, the Nineteenth Amendment to the Constitution finally became law. The deciding vote was cast by Harry Burn, a twenty-four-year-old member of the Tennessee state legislature. Before the vote, his mother had written him a letter. It said: "Don't forget to be a good boy and help Mrs. Catt." He did just what his mom told him to do!

POLITICAL PIONEERS

Nineteenth Amendment

The right of citizens of the United States to vote shall not be denied or abridged by the United States or by any State on account of sex.

When this amendment passed in 1920, some people predicted that women would take over American politics. Male politicians did pay more attention to women's concerns, but only a few women were elected to public office. The road to equality, from 1920 to the present, has not been an easy journey. The biggest problem of all may be that many voters—both male and female—are not used to the idea of having women as their political leaders.

Here are some of the political pioneers.

1924

Miriam "Ma" Ferguson (left) and Nellie Tayloe Ross (right) were the first women voted in as state governors.

1932

Hattie Wyatt Caraway (right) was the first woman elected to the U.S. Senate.

1968

Shirley Chisholm (left) was the first African-American woman elected to the U.S. House of Representatives.

1984

Congresswoman Geraldine Ferraro (left) ran as the Democratic Party's nominee for vice president of the United States. Even though the Democrats lost the election, Ferraro proved that a woman could run a strong campaign for one of the top offices in the country.

1992

Carol Moseley Braun (right) was the first African-American woman elected to the U.S. Senate.

For the first time in the history of the United States, women could participate as full citizens. Ever since, women have contributed to the decisions and future of the country. The movement for even more women's rights continues to grow as women take more control over their own lives. Today, many women are politicians. They have careers. They start their own businesses. They are athletes. They work in factories. They fly airplanes. They are lawyers. They are police officers. They are doctors. They are top executives for big companies. And someday—thanks to people like Elizabeth Cady Stanton, Susan B. Anthony, Carrie Chapman Catt, and Alice Paul—a woman is sure to be president of the United States of America.

GLOSSARY

A woman campaigning

campaign – to work on behalf of a political candidate or cause

citizen – one entitled to the full political rights of his or her native country

Congress – the group of elected politicians who make laws for the United States; it is made up of the House of Representatives and the Senate

constitution – the basic set of rules for a country

constitutional amendment – a change or addition to a constitution

Declaration of Independence – the document that proclaimed America's independence from England on July 4, 1776

democracy – a system in which the leaders of a government are chosen by the people

feminism – a political movement focused on women's rights

governor – the top official in each state

politics – activities connected to the affairs of government

Quakers – a religious group, founded around 1650, that believes in equality between men and women

suffrage – the right to vote

suffrage

TIMELINE

1648 Margaret Brent demands right to vote

1776 Declaration of Independence signed

1788 U.S. Constitution ratified

1848 First women's rights convention in U.S.

National Woman
Suffrage Assoc.
and American
Woman Suffrage
Assoc. formed

1869
1870 Fifteenth Amendment ratified

1890 National American Woman Suffrage Assoc.
formed; Wyoming gives women right to vote

National Woman's Party formed **1913**

1916

Nineteenth Amendment ratified **1920**

Shirley Chisholm is first African-American **1968**
woman elected to Congress

Geraldine Ferraro is first woman to run for **1984**
vice president of U.S.

Jeannette Rankin
is first woman
elected to
Congress

INDEX *(Boldface page numbers indicate illustrations.)*

PHOTO CREDITS

©: Cover, The Bettmann Archive; 1, Archive Photos; 2, 3, The Bettmann Archive; 4, 5, North Wind Picture Archives; 7, The Bettmann Archive; 8, Sophia Smith Collection, Smith College; 9 (both photos), 11, The Bettmann Archive; 12 (top), Sophia Smith Collection, Smith College; 12 (bottom), North Wind Picture Archives; 13 (top), The Bettmann Archive; 13 (bottom), 14 (top), Sophia Smith Collection, Smith College; 14 (bottom), New York Public Library Picture Collection; 16 (top), The Bettmann Archive; 16 (left center), Sophia Smith Collection, Smith College; 16 (left bottom), 17 (top), The Bettmann Archive; 17 (bottom), Archive Photos; 18, The Bettmann Archive; 20, Sophia Smith Collection, Smith College; 21 (top), 21 (center right), The Bettmann Archive; 21 (bottom right), Sophia Smith Collection, Smith College; 22, UPI/Bettmann; 23, Corbis-Bettmann; 24, New York Public Library Picture Collection; 25, 26 (right), UPI/Bettmann; 26 (left), The Bettmann Archive; 27 (top right), 27 (top left), UPI/Bettmann; 27 (bottom right), Reuters/Bettmann; 27 (bottom left), 28, UPI/Bettmann; 29, Archive Photos; 30 (top left), The Bettmann Archive; 30 (bottom left), 31 (left), Archive Photos; 31 (right), UPI/Bettmann

ADDITIONAL PICTURE IDENTIFICATIONS
Page 1: A 1912 suffragette parade on Fifth Avenue in New York City
Page 2: Women campaign for the right to vote in the early 1900s.

SUBJECT CONSULTANT
Alana Erickson, Women's Studies Department, Columbia University

ABOUT THE AUTHOR
Miles Harvey is a journalist who has worked for *In These Times* and United Press International. He is the author of several books for Children's Press, including *The Fall of the Soviet Union* and *Presidential Elections* in the Cornerstones of Freedom series, as well as biographies of Barry Bonds, Hakeem Olajuwon, Juan Gonzalez, and Deion Sanders. Mr. Harvey lives in Chicago with his wife, Rengin Altay. This book is dedicated to Mae Fisher, an inspirational feminist and a beloved great aunt.